P9-DTC-611

1/24

MINNESOTA DRAMA EDITIONS NO. 8 • EDITED BY MICHAEL LANGHAM

Sophocles
OEDIPUS THE KING

translated and adapted
by ANTHONY BURGESS
*With Comments by
Anthony Burgess,
Michael Langham, and
Stanley Silverman*

THE UNIVERSITY OF MINNESOTA PRESS
Minneapolis   London
in Association with the Guthrie Theater

Oedipus the King and "To the Reader"
© Copyright 1972 by Anthony Burgess.
© Copyright 1972 by the University of Minnesota.
All rights reserved.
Published by the University of Minnesota Press
111 Third Avenue South, Suite 290, Minneapolis, MN 55401-2520
http://www.upress.umn.edu
Printed in the United States of America on acid-free paper

Library of Congress Catalog Card Number: 72-85784
ISBN 0-8166-0667-6

Seventeeth Printing, 2011

CONTENTS

To the Reader   *by Anthony Burgess*   3

Oedipus the King   9

An Exchange of Letters
between Translator-Adapter
Anthony Burgess,
Director Michael Langham,
and Composer Stanley Silverman
concerning the Production
of *Oedipus the King*
at The Guthrie Theater   81

TO THE READER

TO THE READER

IF THIS IS a translation of *Oedipus Tyrannos,* it is only so in a somewhat Pickwickian sense. With a rusty scrapheap of Greek behind my eyes, I worked on it in no spirit of precise scholasticism but solely out of a desire to create a version suitable for a particular theatre and a particular director. It is always a comfort to know that theatrical effectiveness is the best answer to the screams of outraged purists. In terms of a tradition which still works in the study but is, I submit, shaky in the theatre, I have committed at least one unforgivable sin in this version: I have made Oedipus blind himself in full view of the audience. The Attic aesthetic forbade the presentation of violent action, but it is not easy for ourselves to forget Seneca and the Elizabethan Senecans. To a present-day audience the demand to see what happens, however bloody, has been so long sanctioned by Kyd, Marlowe, Shakespeare, Webster, and Ford that it seems to be a perversion of the aesthetic of the stage merely to recount what happens. Admittedly, Jocasta is not shown killing herself in this version, but we have learned from the Jacobeans not merely the attractions of represented violence but — negatively — the virtues of moderation. Enough

< 3 >

is enough, and Oedipus's sticking pins into his eyes is certainly enough.

There is another reason too for this meddling with Sophocles, and that has to do with the claims of reasonableness. Men whose eyes have just been put out do not, unless they are still under a local anaesthetic, talk reasonably or even unreasonably: they do not talk at all. It seems to me that the agony of Oedipus's witnessing the death of his mother-wife is enough agony to sustain him through one long passage of dialogue; his self-mutilation should properly bring all his capacity for speech to an end: thereafter other forces may take over.

As for my meddling with Sophocles's lines as opposed to his action, the scholar will notice that nothing that he wrote has been taken away, but something has been added. What has been added relates chiefly to anterior action — Oedipus's solving of the riddle of the Sphinx. Most people, though not all people, know what the riddle was, and few, knowing the riddle, find it easy to understand why only Oedipus could solve it. It is a very easy riddle, as one of my child-characters (not to be found in Sophocles) is ready to point out, and one has to find a plausibility for Oedipus's success following the lethal failure of so many others. The point made by one of my "elders" is that the riddle was not meant to be answered, since answering it might be more dangerous than not answering it. It is presumably better to be eaten alive by a monster than to kill one's father and marry one's mother — those consequences of Oedipus's easy achievement that the action eventually reveals. It is to be noted also perhaps that the riddle, though it has a general answer, has a particular applicability to Oedipus in what are known as arithmological terms. We can separate out from four legs, two legs, and three legs a figure of resurrection, since 3 leads on to 4 and resumes a cycle. Oedipus, seeing himself as a creature of unknown parentage, exults in

< 4 >

being a sort of creature of nature, an animal-human member of a family which is itself the cycle of the seasons. But he ends as a kind of mutilated god who helps to keep that cycle alive. In both images he is not unlike the Sphinx.

The relationship between riddle and incest is one that Lévi-Strauss, the high priest of structuralism, has shown to be widespread among the patterns of primitive societies. Thus, Algonquin Indian lore, as well as that of ancient Greece, makes much of the collocation of ability to answer a riddle — invariably put by a creature both human and animal — and a consequent unwilling or nescient impulsion toward the incestuous act. My own imagination was, three years ago, so stimulated by reading Lévi-Strauss that I was led to write a novel called *MF* (or *M/F* or *M.F.*) in which a young man is so good at solving word puzzles that he is drawn, totally against his will, to the commission of incest with his sister. The law which Lévi-Strauss propounds, and which is fulfilled in the Oedipus play, states that the conditions designed to obviate the commission of the act are the very conditions which will bring the act about. Only if one can avoid the confrontation with the dangerous chimerical riddle-asker is one able to save oneself from the crime which, in primitive societies, is so abhorrent that it is associated with the total disruption of nature. Sophisticated societies are more tolerant: Egypt insisted on incest in royal marriages; incest only became a crime under English law in 1908. Nevertheless the taboo has a place in post-Attic literature, and it is interesting to note that it is occasionally associated with riddling—Shakespeare's *Pericles*, for instance, and even Joyce's *Finnegans Wake* (where young Shem is prevented from copulating with his sister by his inability to answer a riddle put by the rainbow-girls).

Why this association between three disparate-seeming elements — the act of incest, the riddle, the animal-human

< 5 >

destroyer? The Sphinx or, in Algonquin legend, the talking bird may symbolize the cursed or holy (*sacred* etymologically meaning both) product of a forbidden union. The riddle may stand for the intriguingly easy but inexplicably forbidden (boy-child and girl-child in bed together, love-play, punishment, why?) or for the knot which holds natural or social order together, untied at our peril though so tempting to untie. I put it this way in my novel: "The riddler has to be itself a riddle. But no: the ultimate organic creation's emissary, rather, granted a voice. With this voice it says: *Dare to try to disturb the mystery of order.* For order has both to be and not to be challenged, this being the anomalous condition of the sustention of the cosmos. Rebel becomes hero; witch becomes saint. Exogamy means disruption and also stability; incest means stability and also disruption. You've got to have it both ways, man." The anomaly or "both ways" means that Oedipus is the cause of the state's disease and disruption but also, through his discovery of and expiation for sin, the cause of its recovered health. He is a criminal but also a saint. In other words he is a tragic hero.

Anthony Burgess

Rome, 1972

< 6 >

OEDIPUS THE KING

Characters

OEDIPUS, king of Thebes

JOCASTA, his wife

CREON, Jocasta's brother

TIRESIAS, a blind prophet

Messenger from Corinth

An old shepherd

An officer of the court

Elders

Children

Chorus of citizens

PART ONE

(*A bare stage, but there should be a simple shrine down left. Before the palace of King Oedipus at Thebes. A chorus representative of the citizenry comes on, with four elders leading a group of children.*)

CHORUS

> Oedipus, Oedipus, king,
> Solver of riddles,
> Slayer of monsters,
> Savior of the people,
> Hear.
> Hear the voice of the agony
> Of the city.
> Leave your palace.
> Come among us.
> Hear.

(*Oedipus comes out toward the end of the speech*)

OEDIPUS

Sons and daughters of the city-state of Thebes,
I was ready for the voice of your supplication.
I do not cling to my kingly right

< 9 >

Of hearing the city's wrongs through messengers.
Messengers distill, abstract, smooth over.
Avoiding violent speech they do violence
To the truth. And there is a truth here
That will not yield to words.
It is in the ears and nostrils —
A stench of decay countered in vain by your incense,
Groans undrowned by holy hymns.
I, Oedipus, whom men have called the Great,
Come not now to you in greatness,
But in humility, as the city's servant,
To hear — hear what? You elders —
Speak for the rest. If it is sickness,
My physicians await; if it is simple need,
My granaries are open. Before you even ask,
I spend pity, dispense compassion.

FIRST ELDER

Ruler of our country, I, a priest of Zeus,
I and my fellow priests, at the shrine of Pallas,
At the temple where the oracle speaks in fire,
Have done sacrifice, have prayed, have led
Others in prayer, crowned with garlands
Of supplication, hair and garments torn,
All over Thebes.

SECOND ELDER

               Your subjects wail,
Wonder, ask why of the gods.
You have seen it yourself already —
Our city, thrashing, heaving, reeling in shipwreck,
Scarcely able to thrust its prow
Up from the surge of blood —

THIRD ELDER

A blight is on our fields and on

< 10 >

The cattle of our fields. A blight
Lies on our women. What children they bear
Are dead or deformed. The fire has struck.
A god that carries fire worries our roofs.
We grow poor while death grows rich.

FOURTH ELDER

Oedipus,
We have not come to you as one goes to a god.
You are no more than a man, though our first of men.
But we remember — and to these children here
It is a lesson at school as well as a bedtime story —
How you came one day and saved this city.
You freed us from the tribute which we paid
In blood and bones to the Sphinx,
The lion-woman with her cruel song, her riddle
Which you alone could answer.

THIRD ELDER

It was said,
And it is said still, that what you did
You did through God's aid, that God
Shone over you then. I and others believe
That God walks with you now.

SECOND ELDER

Though some say
God nods in a chair behind you, or has
His chin on your shoulder, dozing, and that you
Must shake him awake.

FIRST ELDER

Oedipus,
Who helped us in days that grow already fabled,
Give us your strength now. Let not the word Savior
Be a mere formal word struck on a medal,
An empty honorific of dead ceremony.

< 11 >

SECOND ELDER

                              Save us.

A savior is one who saves, not one who
Has saved.

THIRD ELDER

            Find us some means of salvation,
From god or some superior man. We know that
Long knowledge of trials past lends strength
To the acts of the present.

FOURTH ELDER

                        Restore us to life,
Restore our city to life. And, if I may say this,
Look to your honor, your fame. Let none be able
To say that under your rule we were raised up high
Only to fall low.

THIRD ELDER

                  Save the city
And keep it safe. That star that shone over you
In the day of your coming, that gave us fortune then,
Surely must shine still, though in hiding.

SECOND ELDER

If you are to be our king —

ALL FOUR

If you are to be our king,
Be king of the living not
Of dead stone and empty air.
A city is a city, a ship
A ship only when men possess them.
King of nothingness —
There is no kingship there.

OEDIPUS

Need I tell my grief, my brothers, my children?
I know what you suffer, believe me, I know

< 12 >

What you wish of me. You suffer, yes, but
None suffers more than I. For each of you
Is confined to his own grief, but I
Bear the intolerable weight of yours
And that of all my people. I am not blind,
I am not asleep. Sleep indeed is a rare
Visitant. But tears oppress me and the
Wide night is a labyrinth I tread
With no thread of useful thought to
Lead me to the light.
                   But I have done
A little more than weep and wander
In a circle of thought. There was, is,
A source of hope and I sought it. The Lord Creon,
Brother of my queen, has been
Sent to the shrine of golden Apollo, there
To seek of the oracle what word or deed of mine
May help you, may help us all. Today
He is due to return, not long after sunrise
According to his undertaking. Watch for him.
Give me news of his approach. Upon my honor
As a king and a man, all that the god enjoins
Shall be done, shall be promptly done.

    FIRST ELDER

Well spoken.

(*Oedipus leaves. A child speaks.*)

    CHILD

Tell us about the Sphinx.

    SECOND ELDER

You've heard the story too often.

    CHILD

But tell us again.

FIRST ELDER

The Sphinx — she is so far back in the past
As to seem a mere fable, a fairy-tale ogre
To frighten infants. But she existed.
Her body was a lion's body —

SECOND ELDER

Her face the face of a virgin girl.

FIRST ELDER

She ravaged our country, roaring up
To the unwary wanderer in a swirl
Of dust.

SECOND ELDER

       To any she met
She put a riddle. None
Could ever answer it.

FIRST ELDER

            Then
She would leap on the ignorant one
And eat him.

CHILD

         What was the riddle?

SECOND ELDER

You know the riddle, you all
Know the riddle.

FIRST ELDER

         Bear with the child,
Bear with the children.
They all love to hear it
And answer it. Each of them gains that way
A little of the substance of Oedipus.

SECOND ELDER

Very well, then. Which animal
Walks on four legs in the morning,

< 14 >

Two legs at noon, and three legs
In the evening?

CHILD

The animal is man.
As a baby he crawls on all fours.
In the noon of his life he walks
Upright on two legs. And in old age
Or evening he walks with a stick.
It's an easy riddle.

FIRST ELDER

Easy or not, not one could solve it
Except our king. Trudging toward our city,
A stranger, unknown, seeking his fortune,
He met the Sphinx and answered
The unanswerable. In chagrin
She killed herself, our scourge was gone
And, as a reward, Oedipus our lord
Gained the crown and the hand
Of our widowed queen.

CHILD

And yet it's an easy riddle.

SECOND ELDER

The point about the riddle was
That it was unanswerable.
Difficult or easy — that was never the point.
The riddle was unanswered because
It was unanswerable.

CHILD

Why?

FIRST ELDER

He is coming. Creon is coming.
Call the king.

(*One elder goes in to fetch the king. The others call.*)

< 15 >

CHORUS

(*severally*) Oedipus — King Oedipus!

(*Oedipus enters*)

THIRD ELDER

Creon is smiling. The news is good.

FOURTH ELDER

He has crowned his head with ripe berries
Of the bay tree. The news must be good.

OEDIPUS

Welcome to our royal brother.

(*Enter Creon*)

Creon,
The times, our agony, your mission — all
Forbid the delay of a private audience,
A public announcement to follow. It is
In the presence of the people that you must
Deliver what comes from God's mouth. Tell us, then:
Is it good or bad news?

CREON

Good news.
Or shall I say that good may come
Even from what seems evil, if things go right.

OEDIPUS

But the answer? What was the answer?

CREON

May I speak before all?

OEDIPUS

The plight is theirs. They have first right to an answer.

CREON

This then is what Phoebus Apollo our lord
Said and commanded. There is something unclean
That was born and nourished on our soil and now
Corrupts and makes filthy our soil. It is

< 16 >

Destroying us. It must be driven away,
Or must itself be destroyed.

OEDIPUS

This is another riddle. What unclean thing?
What manner of expulsion or destruction?

CREON

The unclean thing is a man. The god
Decrees the banishment of a man or else
Or also the shedding of blood.
From the shedding of blood comes our city's agony,
Our city's peril. Blood calls for blood, he says.
Blood must be paid with blood,
Or loss with banishment. Or both.

OEDIPUS

What blood does he mean? Whose blood
Was shed?

CREON

         Before you took the throne, the throne
That I as regent offered to the slayer of the Sphinx,
We were ruled by King Laius.

OEDIPUS

                I know of Laius
Though I never knew him. He died.
That was why the throne was empty.

CREON

Laius was killed. The meaning of the god's command
Is that the unknown killer of Laius be made known;
Made known, be brought to justice.

OEDIPUS

            But how
Is that possible? Where would that murderer be?
It is so long ago. How can we hope to
Trace those buried footprints now?

< 17 >

There was a murder, and that murder grows to a fable
Like the Sphinx herself. Where can we even begin
To look?

CREON

             Here — the god said.
Seek. There is no doubt
That all will be found out.
If blood is not sought,
Blood will not be bought.
Those are the words.

OEDIPUS

When I took the crown from your hands I knew
You mourned a dead king, but I have never yet
Inquired into the precise
Manner of his death. Was it here at home,
Or on the field of battle, or abroad
On the soil of the stranger that he
Met this death, this violent death?

CREON

Laius set forth on a holy pilgrimage
To some distant shrine, some distant god.
And from that day of his leaving he was distant forever.
We never saw him again.

OEDIPUS

                  Did no word come back
From fellow traveler, from retinue
Of accompanying officers or servants —
From any who saw what happened?

CREON

There were servants with Laius. All died,
All were killed with him — except one who
Fled the carnage in terror. He had nothing to tell,
Nothing for certain — except for one thing.

< 18 >

OEDIPUS

One thing would be something — a clue
Pointing to other clues.

CREON

This man's story was
That a band of robbers, not one robber but many,
Fell on the king's party and slew them.

OEDIPUS

Robbers — it seems unlikely. To kill a king.
Unless they were under high orders — orders from here,
High money, protection from on high.

CREON

This too has been thought of. But there was
Much to harass us. Too much trouble in the state
To seek to seek out the murderers or the
Arch-murderer behind them —

OEDIPUS

Is that possible?
Surely no trouble in the state could be so great
As to hinder a state inquiry into
A royal death, a royal murder?

CREON

You forget the Sphinx,
You who slew the Sphinx and delivered us.
The Sphinx was very much alive in those days.
She took up all our attention.

OEDIPUS

We will start,
As from now. We will seek
To bring everything to light that has been too long
    hidden.
All thanks to you, Lord Creon, and all praise
To Phoebus Apollo, for telling us what our duty is

< 19 >

To the dead. Be sure you will find me
Untiring in this cause — God's cause,
Our country's cause. My own cause also,
Since it is from myself as well as my subjects
That this stain must be cleaned away. After all,
The killer of Laius, secure in his ability
To kill a king and go unpunished because
Undetected — might he not, whoever he is,
Turn against this king?
Serving the cause of Laius, I serve myself.
People of Thebes, there is nothing I will not do
To douse the fire, to smite the demons,
Deliver our city, with God's help, from the
Blood that is bred of blood. Now let me
Enjoin you, the faithful, to show your faith.
Pray to the gods for guidance, revelation,
The lifting of the curse. That they
May bless you is my own prayer. I take my leave.
(*He and Creon go into the palace.*)

FIRST ELDER

Come, children. You have heard the voice of the king.
He has promised us all that we came to ask.
Let us go and add our prayers to his efforts,
That we may be saved.

CHILDREN

        Oedipus, Oedipus, King,
        Solver of riddles,
        Slayer of monsters.
        Seek out the monster
        That killed a king.
        Answer this riddle,
        Unwind
        The tangled string.

< 20 >

(The first elder takes the children away. The remaining elders mingle with the chorus, which is now totally adult. The chorus chants.)

CHORUS

Strophe

To Thebes, the city of light, from out of the gold
Shrine of the golden god the word has come.
It is not a word of deliverance that is told.
Fear cleaves our hearts, fear renders us dumb.
Hear, O hearer, healer of Delos, hear,
Tell us in our fear what you will do.
Will it be something new?
Will it be something old as the wheeling year?
Daughter of hope, we call on you.

Antistrophe

There are three divinities
Whose task it is
To avert
Adversities.
Artemis, Artemis,
Daughter of the father of
The gods, who
In majesty but with a special love
Sits above our city.
Next, from her sister Athena, we
Seek pity. Last
From Phoebus, lord of the bow, the far
Shooter, we ask
Aid in our task.
O, in the past
You drove away fire, plague, famine
        from the state.

< 21 >

Be great as then,
Help us again.

Strophe

Our sorrows are so many they cannot be told.
Sickness holds the land. The hand is numb
That drives the useless plow. The shepherd's fold
Is stricken. The city soon will become
Empty of life, the ship is beached, its wood
Rotting, rotten. No seed takes hold
In the earth or in the womb. Like flocks of birds
The hopeless leave the city, seeking some good
On the shore of an alien god. Words,
Words of prayer are all that is left to us,
But our mouths grow cold.

Antistrophe

Death in the streets,
Children lying
Dead in the streets, spreading
Contagion of death.
The breath of the mourners,
The suppliants, freezes
On the altar. Alter
Our condition, Golden Athena,
Golden Apollo, grant
Remission to our pain.
The night wind,
The morning breeze is
Sour with pain.
Once you listened.
Listen again.

Strophe

There is war, but not a war of brazen shields,

< 22 >

No clash of armor lifts the heart. Our war
Is with the god of war himself. He strikes our fields,
Our homes, a savage god, a god of fire, whose roar
Is louder than the cries of the dying. O Zeus,
Exile the war god to some northern shore,
For we can no longer abide the tortured night,
The agony of the morning. Let your bright
Lightning strike him, turn loose
Your steeds of thunder under whose fiery feet
He will be beaten and crushed and seen no more.

> Slay him, Apollo,
> You of the golden bow.
> Artemis, slay him, flashing
> In torchlight
> Over our hills. And you,
> Bacchus, splashing
> Wine in boisterous revelry,
> With your torch of pinewood
> Scorch him, burn him,
> Send him screaming away,
> The enemy,
> The god whom all the gods
> Abhor and loathe to see,
> Restoring joy
> To the bright day!

(*Oedipus comes out from the palace*)

OEDIPUS

You have prayed, and your prayers will be answered
If you will but hear my words and obey them.
A remedy is at hand and we must
Put it in hand. Listen to me now
With close attention. Though your king,
I am in many ways a stranger — a stranger especially

< 23 >

To the story of Laius's death as much as to
The black deed itself. I need a beginning,
A fact, the start of the thread which will
Lead me through the labyrinth. Therefore,
A citizen speaking to his fellow citizens,
I ask you, Thebans: if any of you knows,
If any of you thinks that he knows who the
Murderer of Laius was or is — let him speak.
Let him declare the truth fully to me —
In public, or in secrecy if he wishes.
(*There is no reply*)
Let me say more. If any man's conscience is guilty,
He may give himself up without fear. His fate
Will be instant banishment, no more.
He who was merciless shall know the taste of mercy.
(*silence still*)
Or if it was some foreigner you know
To have been the assassin, declare this openly.
The informant shall be rewarded, not only with thanks.
(*silence still*)
But — let me speak plainly — if one among you
Is found to be hiding himself or another in fear,
In lack of faith in my clemency, I here
Pronounce his sentence. Whoever he be,
I forbid him shelter in my land, the hand
Of human friendship, the comfort of
Religion, of prayer or sacrifice or the right
To the lustral rites of cleansing. I hereby
Excommunicate him. He shall be totally
Homeless, friendless, godless, cursed and unclean.
I follow the divine oracle in this, doing
My duty to the god as well as to the dead.
And I pray in all solemnity that the

< 24 >

Unknown murderer and his accomplices,
If accomplices there be, shall wear
The badge of shame, the brand of infamy
On the very skin to life's end, world's end.
I seek no royal exemption from this curse.
If, in full knowledge, I have harbored
In house, on hearth, this man of blood,
Then on my head lie the evil and the
Consequences of the evil. We have, all of us,
A duty to see that these duties to the god,
To our suffering country, be faithfully carried out.
A stranger in so many ways, I am a stranger
In my failure to understand why, when he died,
Your late king, there were no voluntary acts
Of purification — acts unprompted by the gods, I mean.
So good a king — his death went by
With no more perturbation in the state
Than might be occasioned by the death of a beggar.
I cannot understand why the most
Rigorous inquiries were not undertaken.
So good a king. But enough of this.
I stand in his place, having inherited
Not only his crown but his bed,
His dear wife, now my dear wife.
Had there been children of his, they would have been
A further bond of blood between us.
But there are enough bonds. His cause is mine.
I will fight for him as I would fight
For my own father. No corner of the labyrinth
Shall lack the probing of light till the light bring forth
The slayer of Laius,
Laius, the son of Labdacus, the son of
Polydorus, the son of Cadmus, the son of Agenor.

< 25 >

The curse of the gods light on all who
Disobey our royal charge. May the earth
Be empty of seed for them, and empty of seed
The women they lie with. May the curse of heaven
Pursue them to the gates of hell. For you,
My friends and brothers, brothers in suffering,
May justice be your ally, may the gods
Grant blessing.

CHORUS LEADER

                    I speak, King Oedipus,
But only to ask. If the god Apollo said so much,
Why cannot he say more?

OEDIPUS

                           I do not quite —

CHORUS LEADER

If asked, would not the god
Say who the murderer is?

OEDIPUS

One does not ask again. The god's silence
Would be a rebuke and a new disappointment.
There is no path there.

CHORUS LEADER

                    I have another thing,
A second thought.

OEDIPUS

                  Second, third — let me have them all.

CHORUS LEADER

Tiresias — I was thinking of Tiresias. He, it is said,
Stands nearest to Phoebus Apollo. The divine fire
Burned out his eyes and killed his manhood, so they say.
For the rest, he withstood it, and
It stays within him.

< 26 >

OEDIPUS

So they say, and for that reason —

CHORUS LEADER

He surely could help more than any in the state.

OEDIPUS

For that reason, I say, he has been sent for.
It was on Creon's advice. I stressed the urgency.
He should be here now to meet me.

A CHORUS MEMBER

Tiresias?

CHORUS LEADER

A bundle of myths, and very old.
And very irritable.

CHORUS MEMBER

Blind, you said?

CHORUS LEADER

So many stories. He was believed to have seen
The goddess Athena bathing. A deadly sin
And he lost his sight for it. Or so some say.
Some say that the gods took pity and
Gave him in recompense the power of prophecy.

ANOTHER CHORUS MEMBER

He has another gift too, they say, unless
It was really a calamity of birth.

CHORUS LEADER

You mean:

He is both man and woman? Who knows?
He is past the pleasures of both, though he may
Suffer with both. There. See the suffering.
See the irritability.

(*Tiresias is led on by a boy*)

OEDIPUS

Tiresias, it was good of you to come.

< 27 >

We know, the whole world knows, that there is
Nothing beyond your sphere of knowledge.
In your heart, if not in your eyes, you see
The wretched state of our city. Only you
Can help us. You will have heard
That we have sent to Apollo for the
Guidelines of help, and Apollo has answered.
The only way of deliverance from the plague
That has struck us is to find the murderer
Of Laius, your late king, and kill or banish him.
Him or them. Sir, your gifts are great.
You have worked in all the modes of divination —
Scrying, astrology, probing the entrails of birds.
Save us, save yourself, you too are of Thebes.
Show us the way of cleansing. To help man
Is the noblest work of man.

TIRESIAS

Very wise words.
But when wisdom brings no profit to the wise,
Wisdom is a mode of suffering. Why did I forget this?
I who knew it so well. It was useless to send for me.
I should never have come.

OEDIPUS

This is no help.

TIRESIAS

Let me go home. It will be easier, believe me,
For you to bear your suffering, me mine.

OEDIPUS

You are great in Thebes, but you show yourself
No friend of Thebes if you refuse to answer.
Son of Thebes, it is the king of Thebes who speaks to you.

TIRESIAS

I refuse to answer, yes. Refuse because

< 28 >

Your words tend to no good. So I guard my own.

OEDIPUS

You know something, yet you refuse to speak.
Let this king be a beggar and beg again.

TIRESIAS

Beg in vain. You sin by asking. I will not
Divulge my heavy secrets — your heavy secrets.

OEDIPUS

More riddles. All I take your words to mean
Is that you know and will not tell. All I take
Your intention to mean is that you will fail us,
See with your blind eyes the city perish.

TIRESIAS

I wish to spare you, I wish to spare myself.
Ask nothing more. I will tell nothing more.

OEDIPUS

Nothing? This is insolence. You would lash
A heart of stone to anger. You are obstinate
Like stone. I command you to speak.

TIRESIAS

Your anger is misplaced. Reserve it
For yourself. Put your own house in order.

OEDIPUS

You hear these insults? My anger is
The anger of the state. It is the state
You insult.

TIRESIAS

         Things will be
As we shall see. Fate's engine
Is beyond the control of man's hands.
You need no prophet to tell you this.

OEDIPUS

What fate will bring to birth —

< 29 >

It is your art or trade to know this
And to say it. Practice your trade.

TIRESIAS

Prepare what new rage you will,
You whose great fault is rage,
I say no more.

OEDIPUS

If you want more rage you shall have it.
I speak openly, I say unflinchingly
What I must now believe. I believe that you
Had some hand in the plot to kill a king.
If you had eyes, I would say that those eyes
Instructed the hand. I say that
In your darkness murder coiled and writhed.

TIRESIAS

You would say that? Very well then, hear.
You have stung me out of silence. On your head
And your head only let the curse fall
That fell from your own lips. You are excommunicate,
Cut off from men. Speak no more to me or any. It is you,
You who are the defiler of this land.

OEDIPUS

You dare to say this? You — shameless,
Treacherous — you know the consequence —
You think you can escape the —

TIRESIAS

                                        I have
Already escaped. The truth is my door.

OEDIPUS

But — it is treason. Who put you up to this?

TIRESIAS

You were, shall I say, the instigator.
You asked, you taunted, you stung. What I said

< 30 >

You made me say. It was against my will.

OEDIPUS

Say it again. Say what you said
Against your will. Let me be clear, let there be
No mistake.

TIRESIAS

        It was plain enough.

OEDIPUS

                Say it loud,
I will know it beyond all doubt. Say it once more.

TIRESIAS

I say that the murderer you seek
Is yourself.

OEDIPUS

      Madman —

TIRESIAS

             It is your voice
That grows to the voice of a madman. Now I have started,
At your request, at your order, remember that —
Will you hear more?

OEDIPUS

          Spew all your madness out.
Fly to the limits of treason. You will suffer.
Say all you know.

TIRESIAS

         This I know. This you do not know.
Your marriage is a sin. Your love is a sin.
Your bed is stained with sin.

OEDIPUS

           Impunity —
You think your blindness and age grant you —

TIRESIAS

The truth grants it, not I, the mere

Bearer of the truth.

OEDIPUS

Bearer of lies, infamy,
Blind, senseless, brainless —

TIRESIAS

Cast no taunts,
You who must yet live in a thunder of them,
Swim in a torrent of them —

OEDIPUS

Do not threaten me,
You, who lack power to make flesh and blood of threats,
You who live in the dark. But men in the light
Lack equal power. My throne is of rock.

TIRESIAS

Rocks, you mean. Your throne rocks. No, I admit
I cannot harm you. But the gods can. Apollo can.

OEDIPUS

Apollo — Creon — it is Creon, then? Creon —
His idea, not yours — ?

TIRESIAS

Creon is not your enemy.
You are your own.

OEDIPUS

The shadow of success
Is always envy. It is the scorpion over the royal bed,
The headache under the crown. Creon, my friend,
Trusted so long, standing in the shadow,
With the claw of dispossession ready to strike —
Is it possible? I took the crown from his hand,
A crown unsought by me, freely given
By him. And now — is it possible? —
He sets this cheating monger of magic on to me,
The light of cupidity in the blind eyes.

< 32 >

You, sir — I call your craft into question.
That famous gift was notably lacking when
The Sphinx fed on Theban flesh. That riddle
Which none could answer save I — surely a seer,
A prophet, a special being walking under
The equivocal canopy of the gods, surely he
Should have answered it? But the stars were silent,
The lees in the wine cup yielded no pattern,
The flight of the birds spelled nothing. I,
I, Oedipus, ignorant Oedipus gave the answer
And stopped the riddler's mouth forever,
With no benefit of the prophet's lore. I,
Oedipus, whom you would now dispossess
To feel in your blindness the embossed gold
Of a royal counselor's chair. Tiresias,
Though blind, the seeing eye of Creon.
Make no mistake, you shall regret this,
Creon shall regret it. To make me, your king,
The sacrificial goat — such impiety to the gods,
Such treason.

CHORUS LEADER

            King Oedipus, we hear too much anger
On both sides. If I may say so, the true impiety
Is to waste time in anger, to neglect
The command of Apollo.

TIRESIAS

                 I accept that you
Wear the crown and stand above me, but I claim
No less than what you claim — the right of speech.
Moreover, it was more out of courtesy that I came
Than from a subject's duty. I am not your subject.
Apollo is my one master, him I serve.
Nor is Creon my patron. I answer freely,

< 33 >

As a free being should. You mock my blindness.
First think of your own. You have eyes
That can see and will not. You shut them to
Your own state of sin and impending damnation.
Ask yourself whose son you are. Consider that
A man sins no less for being blind to his sin.
The curse of a father and a mother will yet
Send you packing from this palace and from this land.
Then you shall be blind like me but lack no voice
To cry aloud the horror of the truth
I know but you are yet to learn. Believe me,
You who use your voice to decry
Creon and myself, you shall be struck dumb yet
Before you find the air for lamentation.
You shall be stamped in the ground
But bear no fruit other than bitterness,
The bitterness of men's scorn.

OEDIPUS

I have stood enough. Leave me. Go back
Whither you came.

TIRESIAS

                I came at your bidding,
Not from my own wish.

OEDIPUS

                  If only I had known
What slanderous madness I was to listen to,
I would have spared us both the trouble.

TIRESIAS

You talk of my madness. It is not the word
Your father would have used.

OEDIPUS

                Would have used?
My father lives.

< 34 >

TIRESIAS

     Today you find your father.
Today you are born. Today you die.

OEDIPUS

         Riddles.

I am sick of riddles.

TIRESIAS

      Strange words from a man
Whose pride lay in solving them. But, as you
Shall learn, what was your pride must be your ruin.

OEDIPUS

Ruin, ruin. Let us think of the city's ruin.
I saved it once. I will again. I am Oedipus.

TIRESIAS

And I am going. Give me your hand, boy.

OEDIPUS

Give it, boy. We can well spare him.

TIRESIAS

Wait. This is the last time you will see my face.
The rest of you will see and will remember.
Remember these words. This is the man you seek,
The killer of Laius. He passes for a stranger
But, as he will know to his cost, he is Theban born.
He came here seeing. He shall go blind.
He is rich now, but will soon beg his bread.
A stick shall tap his way into exile.
Where he enters, he once came out.
For the ones he loves, new names are needed,
Names against nature, sphinx-names.
He laid his father low to sleep in his bed.
Remember these things. Blind you called me.
You will not call me blind when you learn to see.
And when you learn to see, it is you —

You who will be blind. Lead me away.
(*He goes. Oedipus enters the palace.*)

Out of the rock of golden Apollo
A voice calls: where is the slayer,
Where is the doer of a deed without a name?
Phoebus, sweet singer, golden harp-player,
Strike strings no longer. Follow, follow
With swift wings, with avenging flame.
The hunt is up. A man in hiding
Skulks in caves, roams the wood,
Lonely as the mountain lion or the wild ox,
Cut off from kindliness, bereft of good.
In every shadow his pursuers are striding.
He whimpers through the snow like a maimed fox.
Tiresias the prophet has unleashed terror
Into our darkness, but darkness it remains.
We lack knowledge, but we do not lack fear.
We ask and hear no answer, beating our brains.
Soothsayers are so often the sayers of error,
Surely it was ghastly error that was spoken here?
The gods know all, but men know so little,
Even the greatest of prophets. Prove blame
On our king and then we will believe.
We stand aghast, aghast at the frail and brittle
Fabric of accusation we watched him weave,
With sure fingers in his blindness. But can that shame
Really attach to our king, whose goodness is a flame,
Whose wisdom is wonder? We will wonder and not grieve,
Unbelieving that the deed without a name
Came from his hand, continuing to proclaim
His goodness, wisdom, trumpeting his fame.
(*Creon comes on toward the end of the chorus. He is angry.*)

< 36 >

CREON

Citizens of Thebes, it has been brought to my knowledge
That the king, King Oedipus, has laid
A most serious and slanderous accusation against me.
I come to you, my brothers, in anger and sorrow.
To think that he should harbor such a thought,
The thought that I have sought his harm, in
Word or act. I do not wish to live
In the odor of such scandal. If you, my friends,
The voices and ears of my country, are, like him,
Ready to cry treason, then I will end it now,
A life already too long.

CHORUS LEADER

           My lord Creon,
Our king is distressed. Take it that his words
Were spoken in an anger so great
It seized on the first object, one close to him,
One dear to him.

CREON

           Enough of that. Did he say
What I heard that he said: that under my prompting
The prophet Tiresias lied?

CHORUS LEADER

           I must admit
That he cried out in those terms — but
With what intention I cannot say.

CREON

Spoken directly, coherently, deliberately,
With none of the stumbling of distress — was this so?
Was the accusation clear and unequivocal?

CHORUS LEADER

Who am I to say more of the deeds or words
Of our master? He has heard you. He is here.

< 37 >

Let him speak.

(*Oedipus comes from the palace and confronts Creon*)

OEDIPUS

You, sir, you have the effrontery to stand in
The shadow of my door, brazening it all out,
Pretending sanctimonious shock, as I
Heard and now see, when you are the
Proved plotter against my life, the
Foiled thief of my crown? For God's sake,
Did you take me for a fool or a coward
Or one lacking eyes like your precious
Senile confederate? Did you think I lacked means
To uncover a conspiracy as puerile as yours?
A childish plot and a hopeless one. How could you
Hope to succeed without powerful friends or
The backing of the people or, yes, money?
Money wins thrones when talent and virtue fail,
When talent and virtue are lacking —

CREON

You cannot know what you are saying. Listen.
I have a right to be heard.

OEDIPUS

                                        I have a right
To justice.

CREON

                        Judge when I have spoken.

OEDIPUS

Quick to speak and, as I know, eloquent.
You cannot cloud in words what you are —
An enemy, a bitter and cunning —

CREON

                                                First let me tell you —

< 38 >

OEDIPUS

Anything you will, except that you're not
Guilty.

CREON

      If you think that unenlightened obstinacy
Will do you any good —

OEDIPUS

                And if you think
That you're safe from justice just because
You're a kinsman —

CREON

                Would I be such a fool?
Why are you such a fool as to think it?
Enough of this nonsense. Tell me — I've a right to know —
The precise nature of the harm I'm supposed to have
   done you.

OEDIPUS

Was it you, or was it not you,
Who persuaded me to send for that
Prophetic humbug, that canting mumbler?

CREON

If you mean Tiresias, yes.
And I would do it again.

OEDIPUS

Doubtless. Now then, tell me —
How long ago is it that Laius, King Laius —

CREON

Laius? What has Laius to do with it?

OEDIPUS

How long is it since Laius — disappeared,
Died, was murdered?

CREON

That you should know, common knowledge.

< 39 >

A little longer ago than your crowning,
Your marriage. The event's a year older
Than your eldest child.

OEDIPUS

Was Tiresias at his profession then,
If you can call it a profession?

CREON

He was an honored prophet.
As honored as now.

OEDIPUS

               In those days,
Did he ever — mention me?

CREON

Not to my knowledge.

OEDIPUS

                 Was there
No inquest into the king's death,
No search for his body?

CREON

We inquired, we searched. There was nothing.

OEDIPUS

And why was our professional wise man,
Our state soothsayer, so silent then?

CREON

I don't know.

OEDIPUS

           You don't know, but
There is something that you know.
And you'd be wise to confess it now.

CREON

I will always confess what I know.
What do I know?

< 40 >

OEDIPUS

This —

That Tiresias would not have said,
Said to my very face, that I
Was the murderer of Laius, if you, sir,
Had not prompted him —

CREON

If he said that, you know best that he said it.
But, since you've pounded questions at me,
Give me leave to ask you something.

OEDIPUS

Ask all you wish. You will never prove me
Guilty of Laius's murder.

CREON

Leave that.

Answer this: are you my sister's husband?

OEDIPUS

You know I am.

CREON

Is she your equal partner
In the rule and revenues of the kingdom?

OEDIPUS

This you know too.

CREON

Do I share your honor?

Am I an equal partner? '

OEDIPUS

Yes, you are,

And being so you are all the more a traitor.

CREON

I deny it, and I could be hot in the denial,
I could counter-rage. But I prefer reason,
And I ask reason from you. Consider this:

< 41 >

I have royal rank, royal honor, but I lack
One thing I am glad to lack — I mean
The unquiet head of a king, the specious
Glint of the crown. I do not wish
To be king — what more could it give me?
Certainly my sleep would be uneasier,
The night shadows more full of menace.
No, I have what I want — royalty and rule
Unqualified by the final responsibility.
Would I not be a fool to snatch from you
The thing I am — selfishly, if you wish —
Least disposed to possess? I have honors enough.
I am liked, I am friend to all men. It is to me
That suppliants for your help or favor come.
Who would seek to exchange this comfortable life
For yours that is so comfortless? Treason?
If you want treason look elsewhere for it,
Among men who grope for power. I have power.
All you need do, you on whose face doubt rides,
Unslowed by reason, is to go yourself
To the shrine of Apollo. Ask if the message
I brought back was the message given. Do that first.
Then I am ready, under due process of law,
To be proved guilty or innocent of any
Conspiracy with our state soothsayer.
If I am guilty let me choose
My own mode of death. It will be far more terrible
Than any that our statutes hold for treason.
Hold me to this, citizens of Thebes.
But I will not be charged in this manner,
On suspicion, on blind suspicion,
Hissing and writhing behind my back. You, sir,
Are guilty of two crimes. The first is little,

< 42 >

Compared with the other — it is this dreary crime of slander.
But the other crime is inexcusable in a king —
The crime of mistaking a good man for a bad.
Throw away a friend and you throw away
Your own life. Time teaches this, but the lesson is a
Long and slow one. Years prove the good man;
The evil man is known in a single day.

CHORUS LEADER

Listen to those words, King Oedipus.
Slow thoughts aim best. Anger hits nothing.
Your quickness of temper is a fault
That has undone lesser men.

OEDIPUS

I pride myself on quickness. I was quick
With the Sphinx, when slowness earned others death.
I am quick at countering quick treason.
What must I do — wait till I am in the net
And the rope tightens?

CREON

                                    Be quick then
With your condemnation. What will you do with me?
Banish me, Oedipus?

OEDIPUS

                                    Ah no, no banishment.
Death. Quick death.

CREON

                                    Think. Be a king.
Show me the wrongs I am said to have done or be doing.
Evidence.

OEDIPUS

                    Obstinate still. Reasonable obstinacy.

CREON

I am obstinate in saying you are wrong.

< 43 >

OEDIPUS

I know I am right.

CREON

                In your own knowledge,

Not in the knowledge of the gods

Or of reasonable men. Not in mine.

OEDIPUS

You are a traitor.

CREON

             And if I am not?

If you are wrong?

OEDIPUS

             Kings must rule.

CREON

Not if they rule unjustly.

OEDIPUS

             Do you hear this,

Thebes, my city?

CREON

             Your city? Is she not my city too?

CHORUS LEADER

With respect, sirs — this is enough.

You need a woman's calm. Now you will get it.

The queen, Jocasta, is coming.

(*Jocasta comes out from the palace*)

JOCASTA

Your noise awoke me. Quarreling, quarreling.

Is this a time to shout out private grievances?

You should be ashamed. There are larger issues

To engage our passions — must I remind you?

CREON

None larger than this. Your husband here,

Our lord the king, is engaged in condemning

< 44 >

Me to death.

OEDIPUS

It is true. He is guilty
Of plotting against my life.

CREON

He will not cease
In his wild accusations. I, Jocasta,
The easy-living, who shuddered in your widowhood
When I feared the crown must come to me —

JOCASTA

Believe him, Oedipus. Believe him for your own sake,
For all our sakes.

CHORUS

Listen, O King, consent.
May your anger be spent.
Let mercy flower.

OEDIPUS

Why should I relent,
Repent of the truth?

CHORUS

Truth, like a flower,
Blooms for all men.
You nourish a sour
Weed of your own planting.

OEDIPUS

Do you know what you are saying?

CHORUS

We are saying that Creon swore
His friendship, never before
Showed falseness, said
Falsehood. The betrayal is your
Betrayal. On your own head
Be the crime.

< 45 >

OEDIPUS

> In asking me to relent
> You ask for my own death,
> Or my own banishment.

CHORUS

> Let the breath
> That carried that word
> Be eaten by the wind.
> All we say is that we have heard
> Too much in too evil a time.
> You have sinned,
> King, in imputing sin.
> We are sick of the wrangling
> Of princes. Let mercy in.

OEDIPUS

If it is your wish that I let him go, then so be it.
This may encompass my own end. Nevertheless,
I say yes to your plea. But you have no power
To quell my hate. I hate him forever.

CREON

It is harsh mercy, the other face of anger.
You build yourself a cell, cut off from the sun,
And furnish it with engines for your own
Torture.

OEDIPUS

> Out of my sight. Take your last leave.

CREON

I am going, wrapped in a traveling cloak.
Of injustice woven by your hands alone.
Wherever I go, I walk in innocence.
(*He leaves. Oedipus moves away from him, turns his back.*
The chorus addresses Jocasta.)

< 46 >

CHORUS

>Persuade him, Majesty,
>Of the wrong he has done.

JOCASTA

>How did all this begin?

CHORUS

>Surmise, suspicion, calumny.
>The heat and stress of the time.

JOCASTA

>Each blamed the other one.
>How? For what fault?

CHORUS

>It is best that we take
>The story as done.
>Let us not make
>More wretched
>This wretchedness of our own.
>Best to leave well alone.
>But talk to him, Majesty.

OEDIPUS

Ignorant peacemakers, you will consider
That you have done well. I tremble for the consequences.

CHORUS

>King Oedipus,
>Hear us once more.
>Who are we to wish harm
>To the man who saved us,
>The man who will yet
>Steer us out of the storm?
>We wished good to goodness,
>To rightness of choice.
>Our voice was raised in this cause.

< 47 >

JOCASTA

My brother banished. Surely I have a right
To know the sudden spring of this hatred.

OEDIPUS

Your brother is your brother. But I am the king.
He plotted against me. He put into the mouth
Of that blind old monger of lies that it was I
Who murdered Laius.

JOCASTA

Is it from his own pretended knowledge,
Or from what others have said and he has heard?

OEDIPUS

He kept himself cunningly clean of the accusation,
Using a soothsayer. Could anything be filthier,
More underhand?

JOCASTA

What has shaken you
Is that a soothsayer may speak truth, after all,
May have said truth now, against all evidence.
We are all superstitious. But let me give you
One instance to show that human prophecies
Can dismally fail. To Laius one day I remember,
An oracle uttered a dismal prophecy. It was not
The god himself of course — God forbid
I should think such a thing — but one of his
Least reliable servants. He said to Laius
That he should die at the hands of his own son,
A son to be born of Laius and me.
But the whole world knows what happened.
Laius was killed by robbers, foreign men,
At a place where three roads meet. As for our son —
And there was a son, the prophet was right in that —
In fear of the prophecy, the king gave orders —

< 48 >

It was a terrible thing to do, I had no part in it,
But necessary, I see that it was necessary —
Gave orders to pierce the ankles of the child
With an iron spike and cast him forth
To die on a barren hillside —

OEDIPUS

Pierce his ankles?

JOCASTA

                So he could not crawl
Out of the deadly cold. Laius could be cruel,
But he could not directly kill. A winter night
Was the murderer. The point though is this —
That the prophecy failed. Laius's son
Did not kill his father. Prophecies *can* fail.
What God intends He prefers to show
In His own time. Pay no heed to prophets.

OEDIPUS

My wife, my dear wife — something
Terrifies me. Something in your words.
My mind wanders back then stops,
Fearful to look —

JOCASTA

                Something in my words?

OEDIPUS

You said that Laius was murdered
At a point where three roads meet.

JOCASTA

That is the story.

OEDIPUS

              Where is the place, Jocasta?
Where did it happen?

JOCASTA

                Phocis — the road divides there,

< 49 >

Leading to Delphi one way, to Daulia another.
OEDIPUS
And the news of his death came when?
JOCASTA
As you know — just prior to your coming,
Your crowning, our marriage. What is it,
What is in your mind?
OEDIPUS

          Oh God God,

To do this to me —
JOCASTA

          To do what? What is the trouble?
For God's sake tell me —
OEDIPUS

          Laius —

What did he look like?
JOCASTA

          Tall, about your height.
Older, of course. White-haired.
OEDIPUS

          Is it possible?

To curse oneself in ignorance?
JOCASTA

          You're ill,
You frighten me —
OEDIPUS

          I have a sudden fear
That that blind man had eyes. Tell me one more thing,
Then, God help me, I shall know.
How was he attended — Laius, King Laius?
Many officers? Many servants? A full
Royal retinue?

< 50 >

JOCASTA

There were five men all told,
Including a herald. One carriage for the king.
The details were clear.

OEDIPUS

All too clear. Who told you?
Who told you all this?

JOCASTA

The one servant
Who escaped and ran home.

OEDIPUS

And is he at home still?

JOCASTA

No. When he returned and saw you king,
He said his life was rooted in the old way.
He could not serve a new master. He asked me
To let him leave the service of the palace
And go into the fields to work as a shepherd.
He wanted no more of the city. I let him go.
He was good and honest. He could have
Begged a far greater favor. But
I granted what he asked.

OEDIPUS

Is it known where he is?
Could he be brought here quickly?

JOCASTA

He could.
His hovel is near enough. Why do you want him?

OEDIPUS

I am full of fear. I fear I have spoken too much.
I must see him.

JOCASTA

See him you shall. But

< 51 >

Meantime tell me everything. I am your wife,
I have a right to know.
OEDIPUS
You have the first right.
For the first time now I tell my whole story.
Listen, my dear wife, who, God help us both,
Are, I fear, all too deeply involved. But listen.
My father was a Corinthian — King Polybus —
And my mother a Dorian: Merope was her name.
I, as prince, was held by the citizens of Corinth
To be their greatest next to the king. Until one day
A strange thing happened. There was a dinner,
And a man who'd been drinking too much
Suddenly and insolently said that I
Was not the son of the man I called father.
I was hurt and angry but, rather than show anger,
I kept silence. I went to my parents
And told them what had been said and they
Were quick to quiet my fears, angry in their turn
That such a story should be put about.
But the story was put about, and put about widely.
I did what I had to do, though without
My parents' knowledge. I went to the shrine
Of Apollo at Pytho and asked,
But to that question received no answer. Instead
I was given, without asking, some information
So wretched, so terrible I could hardly sustain
The telling. For the god said I was doomed
To marry my own mother and bring to the daylight
A misbegotten brood, a breed of monsters
That men would shun as they shunned the Sphinx.
Add to this that I must also kill my father,
And there was but one way open to me —

< 52 >

To leave both father and mother, to flee from Corinth,
Never see home again, so that those ghastly
Prophecies should never be fulfilled.
This is what I did. I started
The longest possible journey, and on this journey
I came to that very neighborhood, the place
Where three roads meet. There I encountered
A herald followed by a carriage with a man in it,
A man like the man you described. This herald,
In a surly way, a way unfitted to my rank
Or indeed to anyone's, ordered me off the road.
I refused, then this venerable one in the carriage
Joined in with equal surliness — he even offered
To thrust me bodily off the road. I became angry
And struck the coachman. The old man
Watched for his moment and, as he passed,
Leaned out with a two-pronged goad and hit me
Full on the head. What could I do except
Seek payment in full for the pain and insult?
My stick struck him backwards from his carriage
And he fell out. The others attacked me
And I — need I go on? If this was Laius,
See then what I have done: rendered myself
Hateful to gods and to men. I was born evil,
I am utterly unclean, murderer and polluter
Of my victim's bed. Was it not enough
To have to leave my country in wretchedness,
Never again to see the parents I had at least,
Have at least, spared from the ultimate horror?
The gods have at least saved me from
Parricide and incest, but, for the rest,
They have spent themselves in malignancy.
As for that other — O God, may that day not dawn.

< 53 >

May I be lost to men's sight forever before
That final corruption visits me. But is not this
Enough, to know I am the murderer
Of the man whose crown I wear, whose queen I love?

CHORUS LEADER

Sir, if I may speak — everything depends
On the testimony of the man you have still to meet.
There is surely still ground for hope.

OEDIPUS

That is true. I can hope. I can wait in hope
For the coming of the shepherd.

JOCASTA

But when he comes
What do you want of him?

OEDIPUS

If his story
Is of robbers, of highway robbers, more than one —
That is the point, a plurality of killers —
Then I am safe. But if he speaks
Of a man traveling alone, then the guilt
Points clearly toward one man who already fears,
Already fears —

JOCASTA

But that was always his story,
A story told and retold, now part of our history.
He cannot now go back on it. But even
If in some small point he changes it,
He will never be able to allay my disbelief —
A disbelief I enjoin on you — in prophecies.
A child of mine should kill him: that was how it went.
But it was the child himself that died.
Poor child. Divination, soothsaying —
I would not cross the street to

< 54 >

Hear any of that nonsense.

You're right.
It is nonsense. Let us have hard fact, the record
Of a simple man's mind. Send for him.

JOCASTA

Without delay. Let us go in, out of this
Burning day. Out of the stench of decay,
The distant murmur of laments. Wait, my love,
My lord, and rest while you wait.
You have need of rest.

(*They leave*)

CHORUS

A Chorale

It is enough to love the law proceeding
   Out of high heaven's light,
Born of the Lord, flawed with no mortal breeding,
   A paradigm of right.

Only the tyrant, blown with insolence,
   Dreams of a higher flight.
Seeking the sky but not the light from hence,
   He finds an endless night.

Ambition is a good in kings and princes,
   May heaven prosper it,
When every deed that breeds from it evinces
   The subject's benefit.

But now we fear the radiance may be clouded
   That issues from the sky,
The visage of divinity be shrouded,
   The truth be proved a lie.

< 55 >

The living voice of heaven that we cherish —
    Is it of little worth?
Shall piety and faith and honor perish
    And evil stalk the earth?

Awaken, Zeus, and show your power in thunder,
    Say that the voice speaks true.
If heaven errs, then is it any wonder
    We fail and falter too?
    And know not what to do?
(*Jocasta comes on, carrying a garlanded branch and incense.
A girl is with her.*)
    JOCASTA

Elders of the city, citizens,
It seems that I must do homage
To the gods, and not solely because of
The plague and the other calamities
We suffer together. I may speak freely,
As to a family, I trust.
You must know, then, that the king
Suffers from stress and unwholesome fancies
I can do little to heal, by either
Advice or soothing words. He is too much
At the mercy of man's speech,
No longer, it seems, able to make sound judgments.
These things will pass, but not without
Help from the gods. Help from the gods
I seek, then — first from you, golden Apollo.
Lift our uncleanness, restore to our ship's master
The skill to steer us all to safe haven.
(*A messenger enters*)
    MESSENGER
Great news.

END OF THE FIRST PART

< 56 >

PART TWO

(*As before, but the quality of the light shows it is much later in the day. By the end of the scene night will have fallen. Jocasta comes on.*)

JOCASTA

These things will pass, but not without
Help from the gods. Help from the gods
I seek, then — first from you, golden Apollo.
Lift our uncleanness, restore to our ship's master
The skill to steer us all to safe haven.
(*A messenger enters*)

MESSENGER

Peace on you, madam, and men of Thebes.
I am come from Corinth, seeking the house of Oedipus,
With a message for the king himself.

CHORUS LEADER

This is the palace, the king is within.
That lady is the queen, his consort.

MESSENGER

God's blessings on you and on your household,
Noble lady, worthy of such a man.

< 57 >

JOCASTA

From Corinth, you say?

MESSENGER

A message from Corinth. Great news, I may tell you,
But tinged with sadness.

JOCASTA

Leave the sadness till after. We have
Enough of our own. What is your good news?

MESSENGER

The people of Corinth wish to make
Oedipus their king — king of all the Isthmus.

JOCASTA

But surely Polybus is their king there, unless —

MESSENGER

You have hit on the sadness, madam.
Polybus is dead. Old age has claimed him.
It was a long good life — perhaps sadness
Is out of place.

JOCASTA

            Dead? Oedipus's father?
Dead of mere age? Quick, girl, go to your master,
Tell him the news.

(*Her servant leaves*)

            So much, now, for your oracles.
The father Oedipus fled, fearing to be his murderer —
Dead by nature's stroke, not by his.
Who again can credit these voices, these
Distillations through fallible men?

(*Oedipus comes quickly out*)

OEDIPUS

What is this I hear? What news, dearest Jocasta,
Am I summoned to —

< 58 >

JOCASTA

Listen to this gentleman,
A royal messenger of your own country. Say then
What all this holy prophesying is worth.

OEDIPUS

Who is he? What is his message?

JOCASTA

A royal officer of the court, I take him to be,
Who says your father, King Polybus, is dead.

OEDIPUS

Is this true, sir? Let me hear it from your own lips.

MESSENGER

This is part of my message, the part
You seem most anxious to hear. It is all too true.
King Polybus is dead.

OEDIPUS

By sickness?
By man's treachery?

MESSENGER

By accident. A small
Accident can put an old body to sleep.

OEDIPUS

Of sickness, then. My father, my poor father.

MESSENGER

Sickness and age. He had had many years.

OEDIPUS

So, well then, we see, dearest Jocasta,
How little trust to repose in booming oracles,
In smoke from the sacrificial hearth,
From the pattern of the birds screaming over our heads.
That solemn prophecy — and now he lies,
His body unmarked by any weapon of mine,
At peace in his grave. Unless, unless, of course,

< 59 >

He died of grief at my absence, with an
Old man's longing to see his son. Does that
Make me his murderer? No, the oracle
Spoke of killing, of the shedding of a father's blood.
Oracles are not to be trusted. This
We know now, we know for certain.

JOCASTA

This we knew before. You have forgotten my words.

OEDIPUS

Indeed yes. I was misled by fear.

JOCASTA

Fear no more.

OEDIPUS

              No more. And yet there is one,
One fear more. My mother lives, sleeps
In an empty bed.

JOCASTA

              And you will dream
Of your body's imprint upon it. Enough of this.
Chance is everything, foreknowledge nothing.
Best to live in that knowledge, in lack of knowledge.
Take the days as they come, live easy.
Dreams have been taken for oracles. If you dream,
As many a man has done, of lying with his mother,
It is but a memory of lying with her once
In babyhood. Put off these imaginings.
Let us live.

OEDIPUS

             I would not wish her dead,
A father dead is enough for now. But, while she lives,
Jocasta, I must still travel in fear.

JOCASTA

Take some comfort at least from the bitter news

< 60 >

Of your father's death.

OEDIPUS

There is a small candle of comfort there.
But I still fear the living. I am not safe.

MESSENGER

Fear the living, you say, sir? Whom do you fear?

OEDIPUS

Queen Merope, your queen. Widow of Polybus.

MESSENGER

She is a danger to you? In what way a danger?

OEDIPUS

There was this terrible oracle, known to me,
Unknown to the people of Corinth.

MESSENGER

                                    Can it be told,
Or does some sacred law forbid your
Divulging it to me, a stranger though a Corinthian?

OEDIPUS

It may be told. When I was a younger man,
The oracle of Phoebus Apollo said that I
Must kill my father, lie with my mother.
This drove me out of Corinth. I regret nothing —
I have married happily, raised a family, known
The sweetness of power — nothing save
That long estrangement. It is good
To know the embrace of a father, a mother —

MESSENGER

That fear, you say, drove you away from Corinth?

OEDIPUS

Drove me away from the chance of killing my father.

MESSENGER

That is all over. As for the other fear,
I can make you rest easy.

< 61 >

OEDIPUS

If you can,
You will not find me ungrateful.

MESSENGER

To be honest,
And I have got where I have through honesty,
I had in mind some sort of tangible gratitude
When you return to Corinth, to rule in Corinth.

OEDIPUS

Of course, I had forgotten. But the crown
Must go elsewhere. I will never set foot
In my parents' house.

MESSENGER

No reason why you should not.

OEDIPUS

You are old. The old forget quickly,
Even sometimes while they are being told.

MESSENGER

I know, I know — you mentioned your fear.
But it's any empty one.

OEDIPUS

Empty?

MESSENGER

Yes. Polybus was not your father.

OEDIPUS

Polybus — ?

MESSENGER

Was not your father.

OEDIPUS

He was not my — why then did he call me his son?
Doubting you now, I wonder whether I should not
Doubt you on your other news.

< 62 >

MESSENGER

Doubt all you will. Truth is truth.
It is truth, for instance, that both Polybus and his queen
Longed for a son, but remained childless.
If my manner to you, sir, seems somewhat more familiar
Than is fitting, it is because — doubt this too if you wish —
Because it was from my hands that King Polybus
Received his son. You were given to him by me.

OEDIPUS

Given? What was I? Something you bought for a drachma
From a family rich only in children?
Something you found in a gutter?

MESSENGER

You were found in a wood, a thicket
On the slope of Cithaeron.

OEDIPUS

Found by you?

MESSENGER

               I was a shepherd then. I became
More than a shepherd later.

OEDIPUS

                    I cannot understand
How a child could come to be — exposed is the term.
A child unwanted, left to die in the cold. Whose child?

MESSENGER

Your ankles had been riveted. I loosed you.
A child's ankles, pierced and fettered.

OEDIPUS

I carry the stigma.

MESSENGER

             And the stigma is in your name,
Oedipus. A man's name always means something,
Though the something be lost in time.

< 63 >

OEDIPUS

Who did this to me — my father or my mother?
This I must know.

MESSENGER

      I cannot tell you,
But the shepherd who brought you to me —
He would know.

OEDIPUS

     So it was not you yourself —

MESSENGER

No, I was guarding my flocks. This other shepherd,
He was, I remember, called Laius's man.

OEDIPUS

Laius? Laius of Thebes?

MESSENGER

       Why, yes. This man
Was Laius's own shepherd, or one of them. The chief one.
Kings have large flocks.

OEDIPUS

      Is this man still alive?
Could I see him?

MESSENGER

     This is Thebes,
And I live in Corinth. These people here would know.

OEDIPUS

Do any of you indeed know the man he speaks of?
An old shepherd I take him to be. Has he been seen
In the city or the pastures outside the city?
For God's sake speak if you know.

CHORUS LEADER

I think he is none other than the one you
Have already demanded to see. But the queen
Surely can best tell you.

< 64 >

OEDIPUS

Jocasta,
You know the man we have sent for. Is it the
Same man?

JOCASTA

(*frightened*)

Does it matter? Is it worth while
Probing into the past, defiling the present?

OEDIPUS

I must follow the clue to the end,
To the heart of the labyrinth.

JOCASTA

In God's name I beg you — no. If you wish to live,
Do not go on like this. Have I not
Suffered enough?

OEDIPUS

Courage, Jocasta. It is a
Matter of my honor, not of yours. If I am proved
To be the son of a slave, of slave's stock
To the third generation — you are what you are.
Your lineage is not brought low.

JOCASTA

Don't do this.
I beg you. Be persuaded by me.

OEDIPUS

I cannot.
I must bring this whole thing to the light.

JOCASTA

It is for your own good —

OEDIPUS

My own good.
If ignorance is for my own good, then I
Want no more of my own good.

< 65 >

JOCASTA

                         Oh, God help you.
God keep you ignorant of who you are.

OEDIPUS

Go, someone. Bring this shepherd to me.
As for our lady the queen, leave her to bask
In her pride of birth.

JOCASTA

                    Lost. Condemned.
What more can I say? Go forward to your
Damnation. There is no turning back now.
I have no more words. I have spoken
My last word.

(*She leaves, terribly distraught*)

CHORUS LEADER

Why, sir, does she go in this grief?
She leaves us the thought of her silence.
What wild beast will rush out of this silence?

OEDIPUS

Let it rush out. Let the silent world,
Silent too long, spew out its secrets.
I must unlock this last door to the last room
Where I myself am lodged. I must look on myself.
What I am or may be already shames her,
The high-born woman. Let it come out.
At worst, I am the son of the goddess Fortune.
Who would not have such a mother? I am
Kin to the seasons — four-legged spring,
Summer upright in its pride, tottering winter.
I rise and fall and rise and fall with the
Rising and falling and rising year. This is my breed.
I ask no other. I am not ashamed
To ask who I am. I will know who I am.

< 66 >

CHORUS

The secret will out in the full moon —
The secret of our master's birth. The earth
Will sound with it, and one spot of earth
Will be honored above any other —
Cithaeron, mother to our king.
Let new flowers spring on Cithaeron,
Bring honor to Cithaeron.

Was he begotten in a summer noon
By Pan, lover of the mountains? Fountains
Sacred to Apollo saw the act of love, perhaps,
Between our god of the sun
And some favored one of the daughters of earth.
Did Bacchus rejoice in his birth,
His wine-stained hands receiving him in joy
From a nymph on Helicon?
Let new flowers spring on Cithaeron.
Bring honor to Cithaeron.

OEDIPUS

Is this the man approaching? A stranger to me,
But much of an age with this Corinthian messenger.
Is it the man?

CHORUS LEADER

                    It is. Well-known to us all,
Laius's shepherd, faithful in his service,
A good man.
(*An old shepherd is brought in by two of Oedipus's men*)

OEDIPUS

Now, sir, you, our friend of Corinth —
Is this the one you spoke of?

MESSENGER

                    This is the one.
It has been many years, but — this is the one.

< 67 >

OEDIPUS

Old shepherd, look at me and listen.
You were, I hear, a servant of King Laius.

SHEPHERD

Yes. A servant but no slave.
Reared in the king's own house.

OEDIPUS

You have always been his shepherd?

SHEPHERD

Most of my life I have tended the king's flocks.

OEDIPUS

In what part of the country?

SHEPHERD

Many parts.

OEDIPUS

Name one part.

SHEPHERD

Cithaeron — and the places near to Cithaeron.

OEDIPUS

And in Cithaeron you knew this man, did you not?

SHEPHERD

Who? Him? I don't know. What was his trade?

OEDIPUS

Forget the trade. You had dealings with this man.

SHEPHERD

It's so long ago — I can't remember.

MESSENGER

It *is* a long time ago. But wait, sir.
I'll make him remember. Don't you remember
A shepherd neighbor on the slopes of Cithaeron?
You had two flocks — I one only.
We had three seasons together — spring to fall.
I would fold my flock in Corinth for the winter,

< 68 >

You would drive yours to Thebes, to the steadings
Of King Laius. Surely you remember?

SHEPHERD

A long time ago. But it comes back, a little.

MESSENGER

Then perhaps you will remember the day
You gave a child to me — a baby boy —
To bring up as my own?

SHEPHERD

(*frightened*)

I don't know.
I don't know what you mean. Why was I brought here?

MESSENGER

To see that child. Or the man who was that child.
Here he is.

SHEPHERD

Damn you, fool. Can't you keep your —

OEDIPUS

Come on now. He's spoken honestly.
More honestly than you.

SHEPHERD

I've done nothing wrong.
Why do you look at me as if I've done —

OEDIPUS

It's wrong
Not to answer a straight question. You were asked
A straight question —

SHEPHERD

This one here
Knows nothing about it, nothing about anything.

OEDIPUS

Look, old man, if you won't speak
Of your own free will, we must use
Ways to make you speak.

< 69 >

SHEPHERD

Don't torture me. I'm only a poor old man.

OEDIPUS

(*to attendants*)

Twist his arms behind him.

SHEPHERD

No, no, leave me. What do you want to know?

OEDIPUS

That child. You gave a child to him,

That child he spoke about.

SHEPHERD

All right, I did.

And I wish to God I'd died the day I did.

OEDIPUS

You'll die now if you don't tell me the truth.

SHEPHERD

And if I do, I'll die. I'll die worse.

OEDIPUS

Come on, out with it. You're wasting time.

SHEPHERD

I said I gave it to him, didn't I?

What more can I say?

OEDIPUS

Where did the child come from?

Your home or someone else's?

SHEPHERD

It wasn't my child, if that's what you mean.

It was another man's.

OEDIPUS

Whose?

SHEPHERD

Please don't ask me any more — please —

< 70 >

OEDIPUS

I'll drag the answer out with your tongue.
Whose?

SHEPHERD

      It was a — the child came from the house
Of King Laius.

OEDIPUS

              A slave? Or one of his own?

SHEPHERD

Must I say?

OEDIPUS

      You must say. I must know.

SHEPHERD

It was his child — so they said, anyway.
Your wife, the queen I mean, could tell you
More about it —

OEDIPUS

        She gave it to you?

SHEPHERD

Yes, sir.

OEDIPUS

    Why?

SHEPHERD

      To — to do away with it.

OEDIPUS

To — kill it? To kill her own child?

SHEPHERD

There was this evil spell put on it, sir.
She cried terribly. But there was this evil spell,
You see.

OEDIPUS

    What evil spell?

< 71 >

SHEPHERD

The child was going to kill his own father.

OEDIPUS

But the child was not destroyed.
You disobeyed an order.

SHEPHERD

I couldn't do it, sir. Could you do it?
Could anybody here? I gave it to this one here
Who's so high up now. I thought to myself:
He comes from another country, he'll take him there,
Right over the hills, miles away.
And now you're here, if it is you.
If it is you, O my God. O my God —

OEDIPUS

All out. Oozed out, to the last drop.
There's a sort of joy in it. No more.
No more to fear. No more to —
Oh, what sin. Oh, what unspeakable —
What filth. To see this in a mirror.
The stain on the bed. The wound in the earth,
Festering. My children, my poor children.
The light is stained. Never again.
The last sunset. No more dawns, no noon.
The light shall not be stained
By my looking on it.
There's a knife to be taken somewhere —
Here, the fountain of seed?
But I would still see. No, the light will look.
The light shall not look. No.
The light has seen enough.
(*He totters out. The messenger and shepherd, talking under
the chorus that follows, go out together.*)

< 72 >

CHORUS

What does it mean? What does it all amount to?
Here was a man the world called happy,
Oedipus, pattern of earthly happiness.
Who, after this, can be called happy?
Who would wish for happiness?

Consider his life. Consider his deeds of heroism.
He shot his arrows straight, favored by Zeus.
He saw the Sphinx, foiled and cursing,
Choke in her own blood. He steered our ship,
His arm was strong against disaster.

Our hearts are torn with this story, with this sight
Of affliction unspeakable, for it is our affliction.
We are all Oedipus, but to some heaven is merciful,
Forbidding the unfolding of the pattern
To the ultimate horror, the thing we have seen.

Time sees everything, suffers everything,
Suffers what must now be inscribed forever
On stone unperishable. Curse after curse,
Begetter and begotten cursed. Son of Laius,
Would to God I had never seen you, you
Who were my light and must now be my darkness.

Our king, our king — stamped like ash into the earth.
But the story is stamped forever in our brains,
In our books, in our very loins. It is
Woven into the light of the sky,
Beats in the blood of the yet unborn,
Is with us, is with you. God forgive us all.
(*An officer of the court comes on*)

< 73 >

OFFICER

Citizens of Thebes —

(*He finds it difficult, in his distress, to continue*)

CHORUS LEADER

My lord

High Steward of the Court, we know.

We have heard. You may spare yourself

The distress of a formal announcement.

OFFICER

Heard? You cannot have heard? I have

But just now —

CHORUS LEADER

There can be no new horror.

We have tasted the last of its wine —

OFFICER

Our queen —

Dead by her own hand. Note what I say,

Preserve what happened before the horror

Rushes into full realization and

Makes me tongueless —

CHORUS LEADER

How? How?

OFFICER

She went raging into her bedroom, fell

Screaming onto the marriage bed, tearing

Her hair, her very skin, crying out the name

Of Laius, cursing the bed in which she

Had brought forth children of her own child, she said.

And then Oedipus entered, calling, begging

For a sword to, as he put it, blast to death

The field of such foul sowing. He raved,

Seeking the queen, hammering on her door.

He wrenched the bolts from their sockets,

< 74 >

And fell into the room. There he saw,
And we saw from behind him —

CHORUS LEADER

Courage, courage.

OFFICER

Hanging from a roofbeam, the rope twisted
About her neck, her body circling, circling.
He cried out like a mad thing and used the sword
To cut her down. And then —

CHORUS LEADER

Himself?

OFFICER

He was prevented. He was prevented from
Tearing in his passion what had no more life.
For her to die once was enough. He ripped
The very brooches from her robe, his hands
Are fists about them. But for his own harm,
He has been made impotent. His sword was taken,
He is under guard. He claims his royal right,
He says, to blazon the unclean thing that is himself
Before the eyes of the wronged. I came
To warn you why he comes and of his
Manner of coming.

(*Oedipus enters, distraught, attendants with him*)

OEDIPUS

Let him be cursed, the man who sought
To do good to a dying child, the life-bringer.
I should have died innocent. Here he is,
Sons and daughters of Thebes, your shame,
The author of your pestilence. Cithaeron,
My foster mother, your winds should have blown
Chill on this body, your snows should have
Buried it. You will remember, you will

< 75 >

Carry a curse in your stone barren of grass
And your stunted trees. And you too,
Crossroad in the clearing, at least that forest
Has not been nourished by a father's blood
Spilt by his son's hand. But wayfarers
Will catch a shiver as of an evil memory
And death sits forever on the signpost. Now,
Let me be hidden from all eyes. Let me go hence.
I am unworthy of death, the benison
Of innocent sufferers. Let me wander
And keep my hell alive.
(*Creon enters*)

CREON

                    I, Oedipus,
Must dispose all things, under God.
You must know that I have not come to
Gloat or reproach. Ask nothing yet. First,
Consider that it would be seemly
To hide such grief from the generality.
We must mourn in private. Let him be
Conducted in.

OEDIPUS

             Let me leave now.
I do not wish to enter that house again
That rang with laughter once and is now,
Through my doing, a house of death. Cast me out.
Or do worse, or better —

CREON

                    The gods must instruct me,
I await the word.

OEDIPUS

              You were given the word.
The god pronounced death on the defiler.

< 76 >

Here he stands, though all unworthy of
So light a sentence.

CREON
                    Death or banishment.
But we must await more guidance.
A king is a king.

OEDIPUS
                    A queen a queen.
You, as her brother, will do what is fitting
For her burial and the accompanying rites.
As for me, I entreat you again — let me go.
I will not quit the kingdom. I will return
To the place my parents chose to be my deathbed —
The mountain Cithaeron. I will wait there
Till death comes. As for my children,
Let the boys stay here in Thebes. They will do
Service in good time. But my daughters,
Girls who shared their father's cup,
Ate from his plate, what can become of them?
What men will seek them? The god of marriage
Will turn his back. Let them be with their father.

CREON
Over your children I must claim control.
The disposal of their future is in my hands.
Come, let us go in.

OEDIPUS
                    One prayer at this shrine
That saw so often a united family
Give praise and thanks. Let me go.
A man can do no harm there.
(*He is allowed to move toward the altar. He pierces his eyes
with the brooches he holds in his hands.*)
Dark dark. The sun has burst there
For the last time.

< 77 >

CHORUS

Horror. Horror of horrors.
The eyes of the world are out.
The gods scream,
Finding poison in the wine cup.
The mountains are molten,
The sea blood.
The mounting moon
Turns her face away.
Day will never return.

(*During the above Oedipus is led within, Creon going also.
The stage is lighted only by an uncertain moon.*)

CHORUS

> The night has come. But who will sleep tonight?
>> Only the innocent.
> Yet even children will cry out in fright,
>> Or dream's bewilderment.
>
> The wolves will howl, seeing inside the moon
>> Ciphers of fear.
> In unborn lands, under some distant noon
>> It will be now and here.
>
> But is there not some sweetness to be wrung
>> Out of such bitterness?
> Drive out the sin — so said the prophet's tongue,
>> And drive out the distress.
>
> And so the blind defiler cleanses us,
>> Grants us new sight.
> Restore the savior's crown to Oedipus
>> After this night.

(*We hear a shepherd's pipe. The dawn comes up. An elder
leads in children with votive offerings which they place on the
altar. This goes on until the end of the scene.*)

< 78 >

CHORUS LEADER

You come in some sort of rejoicing?

ELDER

It is early to offer thanks in person
To the king. But the god is always awake.

CHORUS LEADER

You have heard no news?

ELDER

We live away.
Little of the city's news reaches us.
But we have good news of our own.
A cow calved safely. We heard the crying
Of a newborn human child. The blight
Has lifted from one of our fields.
It seems we are to be delivered
From our afflictions. Praise to the gods.
Praise also to the king.
He has found a way.

(*Oedipus, blind, comes from the palace, escorted by his daughters Ismene and Antigone. He makes his exit through the theatre.*)

CHILD

What has happened to his eyes?

CHORUS LEADER

It is a long story. You will hear it some day.

(*to the chorus*)

Creon has relented. He goes into exile
With his daughters.

CHILD

Who did it to him?
He had only one enemy. And that was the Sphinx.
But he killed the Sphinx.

< 79 >

CHORUS LEADER

Perhaps it was better to be killed by it.
The riddle was not meant to be answered.

CHILD

But he answered it. He saved us.
That's the story we're told.

CHORUS LEADER

It is dangerous to answer riddles,
But some men are born to answer them.
It is the gods' doing. They hide themselves in riddles.
We must not try to understand too much.

CHILD

Why?

CHORUS

Citizens of Thebes, this was Oedipus,
A man strong in war, gentle in peace.
God gave him joy, God gave his loins increase.
His happy lot was fire to the envious,
But now the flutes are stilled, the trumpets cease.
Misfortune's waves have crashed, tumultuous,
Over that head endowed with masteries.
He yields to the Destroyer's animus.
A last day is reserved to all of us.
Look to it always. Human happiness
Is not for human error to assess.
Call no man happy till his days surcease,
Till all the gods of pain declare release,
Fate turns her back upon his obsequies,
And happiness may rest with him in peace.

THE END

< 80 >

AN EXCHANGE OF LETTERS
BETWEEN TRANSLATOR-
ADAPTER ANTHONY BURGESS,
DIRECTOR MICHAEL LANGHAM,
AND COMPOSER STANLEY
SILVERMAN CONCERNING
THE PRODUCTION OF
OEDIPUS THE KING AT
THE GUTHRIE THEATER

Rome, Italy
April 11, 1972

My dear Michael,

Very many thanks for your kind letter. I note your points
and enclose a couple of emendations. As for Jocasta's leavetaking
("Lost. Condemned. . . . My last word."), this is, of course,
like the greater part of the play indeed, a fairly close rendering
of Sophocles. I'm scared of touching it at the moment, and I feel
in some ways that the paucity of words and the inner wordless
struggle might be more effective with a good actress than any
build-up of tragic eloquence. However, I'll think about it. The
finale is a major problem. I'm scared of a bacchanal — really
heretical in a tragedy according to Greek tradition, as you know,
and I do need that final reference to the riddle. On the other
hand, all that is needed if you want a more full-blooded choral
ending is a Te Deum based on the simple words — which hence
may be hidden with cymbals, etc. — "Praise to the gods."
Then Oedipus could do his slow entrance, unnoticed, and the
chorus cuts off for the child's comment. This is a musical
matter, I feel, more than a verbal one.

I come now to music. You'll know that in English-speaking
tradition, so far as the Greek tragedies are concerned, sung
choruses have always been taboo. I think there should be singing.

< 83 >

I think it should come in these places: The opening chorus —
in a Greek mode, with flutes and drums only (the Phrygian mode
— E to E on the white keys of the piano). The children's
farewell — in the same style, perhaps the same tune. The first
main chorus should be spoken without musical accompaniment.
The antistrophes require a greater rhythmical drive and should
have drums. *But then*: final antistrophe beginning "Slay him,
Apollo" should have the whole musical works, it should
overwhelm with sonority. The Chorale ("It is enough to love
the law proceeding/Out of high heaven's light . . .") should be
a real Bach-type chorale, recalling one of the *Passions*.
"What does it mean? . . ." not sung at all. "The night has
come. . . ." — sung definitely. The very last choral commentary
might be divided among individual voices, except for the last
few lines. I must leave this entirely to you.

Again my thanks. I'll think and be in touch. Much love to all.

As ever,

Anthony

< 84 >

The Guthrie Theater
Minneapolis, Minnesota
19 April 1972

My dear Anthony,

Thank you so much for your letter of April 11, in which
you outline your attitude toward the kind and use of music in
Oedipus. Both Stanley and I find your approach exciting.

However, it is a strange fact that after studying your text,
Desmond Heeley (who is designing), Stanley, and I all reacted
very differently from what now appears as your total conception.

Far from finding an evocation of a world suited to Bach's
Passions or a Handel oratorio, the powerful directness of your
writing stirred in all three of us a much more primitive feeling.
And we started to work together with this in mind, with results
that we feel are promising.

Speaking for myself, I have worked on your script with my
imagination in much the same way as I would work on
Shakespeare's *Lear* — that is, as if I were interpreting an
Elizabethan writer way beyond his period, going back and
searching for the essence of the prehistoric world of Lear in which
the people could build Stonehenge, not because they were
strong but because they were frightened.

In the case of *Oedipus,* I have been groping not so much
for answers that are purely Greek as for an atmosphere that is
primitive in its overwhelming superstitions and timeless in its
fears and hidden meanings. I have been very conscious of the fact
that no archaeological evidence of the Oedipus legend has, as
you know, been discovered in Greece, but that there is a lot to be
found regarding Akhaton (probably the original title figure who
lived in the Mycenaean Age) in that other Thebes on the Nile.

After much study and reflection, it seemed best to all three
of us not to stick to one ancient culture, but to take whatever was

< 85 >

most helpful from all at our disposal — Egyptian, African, Tibetan, Hebraic, Cretan, and Greek. This has led us to a setting with a texture of battered, cracked, and timeworn rusty steel with only one sophisticated feature — a highly polished marble altar; and to a costume plan that would be a composite of primitive cultural sources. All male chorus, elders and lesser elders — with an assortment of symbolic headdresses, hand props, and instruments — opening the work by performing varied acts of sacrifice (possibly human) — all of which fail to produce results. There would only be three females in the play, Jocasta and the two daughters.

In terms of music, we found ourselves drawn toward Tibetan chants, the Pygmies, Hebraic influences, the Greek Orthodox Church, and Coptic chants.

We did not come by these feelings easily; they were all inspired by your text. Indeed the only conflict with your text seems to occur whenever you make reference to God as opposed to the gods.

I don't wish to be untrue to the Sophoclean pattern — as far as our understanding of it goes, which of course is limited because of the long lapse in any acting tradition. Nor do I wish to be untrue to the pre-Sophoclean myth from which he took his ingredients.

I am keen to know your reaction. If you feel it necessary, Stanley would be available to come and work with you in Rome. Please let me hear from you as soon as possible.

Much Love,

Michael

< 86 >

Rome, Italy
April 22, 1972

My dear Michael,

Very many thanks for that admirable and thought-provoking
letter. Of course, remember, it's already for me anyway
extremely difficult to *see* the text I wrote with any artistic clarity.
It was written in a kind of hypnotic daze, non-alcoholic, with
the Greek to the left and an Italian-Greek lexicon to the right, but
it was stimulated and qualified by my reading for the novel on
Napoleon I'm writing, specifically reading for the Egyptian
campaigns section, where I started to think of the other Thebes
and the sand-buried Sphinx (disinterred by Napoleon), also by
memories of my reading in Lévi-Strauss for my novel M/F,
which is about this relationship between riddle and incest. I think
you're absolutely and brilliantly right to think of a kind of
inspired anachronistic approach, a synoptic gospel of all ancient
cultures. If this will inspire Stanley to produce music of a
strangeness very remote from baroque oratorio, so much the
better. But when I wrote, somewhat elliptically, of a Bach chorale,
I didn't mean a straight baroque pastiche. You mentioned
previously the Stravinsky-Cocteau *Oedipus,* and I had in mind
probably a "wrong-note" or neurotically distorted baroque like
that. I'm prepared to jettison an undue obeisance to Sophocles,
although there's a very great deal of Sophocles in my script. You
can if you wish get rid of the concept of God — which is in
Sophocles nevertheless and is no attempt to impose on his
polytheism an Hebraic concept — and substitute "the gods,"
except for emotional interjections where it has no theological
flavor. Indeed, you can and probably must take the text as a
wholly pliable pretext for the kind of play you want, though for
heaven's sake don't ask me to rewrite because I honestly don't

< 87 >

think I can — I can't recall the very strange atmosphere of the original process of writing, anything new from me would be *wrong*.

My blessing, get on with it, and I know it's going to be the most astounding *Oedipus* ever to hit any stage.

Much love as always,

Anthony

Composer Stanley Silverman, supported by a Ford Foundation grant, went to Rome to work with Anthony Burgess on the script.

Rome, Italy
May 24, 1972

Dear Michael,

Burgess is being most cooperative and is responding favorably to the production ideas. He keeps saying that this will be a "monumental production." He's quite turned on.

The Oedipus myth to Anthony means that riddles should not be answered, because if you do, you *must* commit incest. Oedipus is a child of nature (he doesn't know his parents) and the riddle represents the cycle of nature 4-2-3 leading back to 4 as in 4-2-3, 4-2-3, etc. He told me he based it on a Lévi-Strauss book which we are researching.

As for the play: He *loves* the primitive music (Pygmy, etc.) and would like to write an Indo-European chant to accompany the

< 88 >

sacrifice you planned for the beginning, which would set the tone for the primitivism. (He is turned on to your idea for the opening.)

The following are notes answering your questions and his general comments on the text.

The first speech of Oedipus: He likes "city-state" because it is remote from our government. He asks if incense could be part of the sacrifice.

"God's aid," etc.: God (singular) is referred to in the original Greek, meaning *a* god.

"If you are to be our king . . .": The four elders together can be treated chorally and accompanied by music.

"The Lord Creon": "The Lord" appears before Creon's name so it is not mistaken for "crayon," and he thinks Creon's title should be given.

The Sphinx: Anthony thinks the description of the Sphinx should be accompanied by a high terrifying music and the riddle by a cyclical ostinato (rhythm) that repeats in a circle.

"Seek. There is no doubt . . .": Anthony feels Creon's lines can be supported by music because it is the voice of God. (I am not so sure.)

"Oedipus, Oedipus, King . . .": Anthony likes the Pygmy sound for the children's riddle and the Coptic music for the strophes.

"There is war . . .": He thinks the final strophe should be accompanied by "drums of war." (I do not.)

"Slay him, Apollo": As he said before, this should be loud, violent, and hysterical.

"For my own father . . .": Anthony thinks some music could come in under "For my own father" through the end of Oedipus's speech. I pointed out that we wanted to be very careful "underscoring" speeches.

"Tiresias?/A bundle of myths . . ." He thinks music can be added under the description of Tiresias, from "A bundle of myths" through Tiresias's entrance with the boy.

"You are excommunicate": I asked Anthony about "excommunicate" and he said that the word is from the Greek and Latin and in this case meant banished from the community. I argued that it means something more specific to an American

< 89 >

audience; however, he *favors* that kind of cross-reference. (I will expand on this point later.)

"The sacrificial goat": This is from the Greek and Greek ritual.

"State soothsayer": Anthony has not found anything to replace "state" which he stands by.

"Listen, O King, consent . . .": Anthony thinks that if the chorus sings "Listen, O King, consent" against Oedipus speaking it could sound too "arty." What he had in mind was that it all be spoken (distributed to members of the chorus perhaps) and lyrical music should be played against it. As I write this I get an idea where perhaps the words could be spoken, and the musical members of the chorus could be singing or humming quietly. This way we could establish a choral "cosmos" that could encompass speech and music at the same time. Similar to the Duke's men humming a hymn at the beginning of *Taming of the Shrew*.

"King Oedipus,/Hear us once more . . .": The chorus speaks this as above.

"At a place where three roads meet": Anthony also thinks we should underline this with a sound.

"You have the first right . . .": He likes our idea of sound under Oedipus's long speech (which is why I don't particularly want to do it elsewhere).

The Chorale: Now we come to the key of the argument. It seems that the reason he liked the primitive production idea was that he meant this version to go *anywhere,* providing it underlined Oedipus's sophistication. He was reassured, for example, when the primitive music we were listening to turned out to be sophisticated. He would be genuinely delighted if you placed Oedipus anywhere that you feel fit. One of the casualties of this eclectic-universal approach is always going to be that the work will be filled with anachronisms, as they are in Shakespeare or Brecht, I suppose. Personally, I can accept them, because my music is so filled with anachronisms. This is all leading up to saying that Anthony did not mean, as we first thought, that this version was a grand Handelian oratorio. He thought we would be using elements from everywhere, and when we got here he thought we could naturally slip into a Bach-like chorale. I pointed out that we were able to achieve an "eclectic" variety

< 90 >

of elements but keep it tightly capped under the umbrella of our primitive approach. He confessed it would place a burden on us in dealing with the "lyrics" for the chorale. I told him I would take a whack at a primitive setting of his chorale. He said a Bach-like setting would still be justified. He also said you could cut the second stanza ("Only the tyrant . . .").

"These things will pass . . .": Anthony likes the idea of the overlapping ending.

"My last word. Forever": I remember your talking about Jocasta's last words. In any event Anthony suggests cutting Jocasta's "Forever" (where we have the cry).

"Let it come out . . .": Anthony suggests we bring in the riddle ostinato rhythm under Oedipus's "Let it come out" through the end of his speech.

"The secret will out . . .": The chorus should sing this. I asked him how important the words were, and he said he understood the music would obscure them somewhat. (He does not mind.)

"What does it mean . . .": Anthony has a plot for the spoken chorus (accompanied by rhythm). It distributes the material between the chorus leader—or a soloist—and the full chorus. I can give it to you when I return.

"Horror. Horror of horrors": This chorus should be "choked" and noisy, supported by lots of sound.

"The night has come . . .": This chorus should be sung, as we discussed, quite beautifully. Anthony said you could cut the third stanza ("But is there not some sweetness . . .") if necessary, but he would rather you did not.

Stage direction — We hear a shepherd's pipe, etc.: He likes the idea, now, of "things" coming to life over the last pages, providing they don't burst into a full-scale bacchanal.

"Citizens of Thebes . . .": The final chorus should start spoken (with accompanying sound). Singing can start on "A last day is reserved to all of us."

As I said earlier, Anthony is excited by your production idea, and he believes his version goes with it. He wants me to throw the primitive tapes away and work from myself. In any event, he is happily prepared to leave it to you. Consequently, your idea of treating Anthony as, say, an Elizabethan writer, in order to get

< 91 >

at the primitive core of this project, is brilliant, especially since the "Elizabethan" in question has no objections.

Mary [Silverman] has been invaluable. Besides speaking Italian, she was present during most of the *Oedipus* discussions. I intend for her to talk to you as well.

I found a copy of Pasolini's screenplay for *Oedipus* in English, with pictures of the film. I will send it to you when I return. It is totally Freudian. There is no riddle. The Sphinx asks Oedipus about himself, and he pushes the Sphinx over *in order* to sleep with his mother. The stills are interesting, though, especially the ones dealing with Oedipus's childhood.

I am glad I am here; it was necessary.

Much love,

Stanley

The Guthrie Theater
Minneapolis, Minnesota
20 June 1972

Dear Anthony,

Stanley's European trip seems to have been a kind of blessing to his creative forces. Thank you and Liana for being so helpful and generous. In Paris he was surprised to find the Sphinx on everyone's mind — except of course the Egyptologists at the Louvre. And London provided its own riddles, which he enjoyed.

He has given me a full account of your discussions and of his purely Greek-bounded chats with Xenakis, who seems a sort of Parisian Tiresias. All revealing and stimulating.

< 92 >

I am thrilled at your attitude. I feel no longer awed by doing the work. Hitherto, I must confess I needed faith to believe in directing it *without answers* (stupid, I know, but human). Now I hear the recurrent Pygmy pipe riddling throughout; now I see the child (or children) seeming to know, teasing the adult world, like that lovely, terrifying face of the Sphinx confronting Oedipus (in the Vatican). That child, which is of course not Soph but Burge, looms large as a tantalizing offspring of the Sphinx which you may not have recognized. Riddle with it and it keeps winning, coming back. Maybe it's Andreas [Anthony Burgess's son].

A single practical point which may be useless but I think worth exploring: the Indo-European sounds you've composed for the beginning are overpowering. But they never recur, which makes them finally a prologue effect. Please think seriously about using similar treatment for other moments, especially the antistrophes. The significant names of Artemis, Athena, Phoebus, Apollo, Bacchus could still emerge. Such treatment would provide what in my mind is a needed relief from persistent concentration on the play's loaded statements.

My sensibilities lead me to believe that American audiences can take only so much deeply charged language, and therefore need to be given an occasional breather — music, sounds, action — though still strictly in the mood of your text.

Please let me know your thoughts.

Love,

Michael

< 93 >

Dear Michael,

It was a great pleasure having Stanley here, and we *did* get
things done, I think. And I'm delighted that images and noises
are working with sense at that end. The problem with more
Indo-European (which a cable from Minnesota University Press
has as "indoor European," a delightful idea, like indoor games or
gametes) is that it doesn't exist. I took a chance on using the roots
and inventing the endings in the little chant I did. One gets the
roots — the language was never written down — by comparing
cognate languages, and this is hypothetical and highly dangerous.
I mean, there's no I-E dictionary. The University Press must be
begged and clawed not to put the I-E chant(s) in the printed
text — it/they only work auditorily and must not be chewed over
by captious scholars. Musically they've got to be overwhelming.
Anyway, sighing, I provide you herewith with two more, though
I counsel caution like any doctor reluctantly prescribing perilous
pillulululues.

I long to be there.

Love as always from

Anthony

< 94 >